Pop Art

Susie Brooks

COMPASS POINT BOOKS
a capstone imprint

Compass Point Books are published by Capstone,
1710 Roe Crest Drive, North Mankato, Minnesota 56003
www.mycapstone.com

Library of Congress Cataloging-in-Publication Data
Names: Brooks, Susie, author.
Title: Pop art / by Susie Brooks.
Description: North Mankato, Minnesota : Compass Point Books, a Capstone
    imprint, [2020] | Series: Inside art movements | Audience: 9-14. |
    Audience: 4 to 6.
Identifiers: LCCN 2018060764 | ISBN 9780756562380 (hardcover)
Subjects: LCSH: Pop art—Juvenile literature. | Art, Modern—20th
    century—Juvenile literature.
Classification: LCC N6494.P6 B76 2020 | DDC 709.04/071—dc23
LC record available at https://lccn.loc.gov/2018060764

Editorial credits
Series editor: Julia Bird
Designer: Mo Choy Design Ltd.
Image research: Diana Morris

Image credits:
Front cover. Roy Lichtenstein, Explosion, 1965-6, lithograph on paper, 56.2 x 43.5 cm, Tate, London.© Estate of Roy Lichtenstein/DACS,London 2018. © Tate, London 2018. 1. Roy Lichtenstein, Explosion, 1965-6, lithograph on paper, 56.2 x 43.5 cm, Tate, London.© Estate of Roy Lichtenstein/DACS,London 2018. © Tate, London 2018. 3. Robert Rauschenberg, Bed, 1955, oil and pencil on pillow, quilt and sheet on wood supports, 191.5 x 80 x 20.3 cm, MOMA, New York. © Robert Rauschenberg Foundation/DACS, London/VAGA, New York 2018. 4x 5 Collection/Superstock. 4. Times Square, Manhattan, 1960s, photograph, R.Krubner/Classicstock/Alamy. 5. Richard Hamilton, Interior II, 1946, oil paint, cellulose paint, printed paper on board, 121.9 x 162.6 cm, Tate, London. © The Estate of Richard Hamilton. All Rights Reserved. DACS, London 2018. 6. Mark Rothko, Untitled (Violet, Black, Orange, Yellow on White and Red), 1949, oil on canvas, 207 x 167.6 cm, Solomon R Guggenheim Museum, New York. © 1998 Kate Rothko Prizel & Christopher Rothko ARS, NY and DACS, London. A Burkatovski/Fine Art Images/Superstock. 7. Robert Rauschenberg, Bed, 1955, oil and pencil on pillow, quilt and sheet on wood supports, 191.5 x 80 x 20.3 cm, MOMA, New York. © Robert Rauschenberg Foundation/DACS, London/VAGA, New York 2018. 4x 5 Collection/Superstock. 8. Edouardo Paolozzi, Meet the People scrapbook version Bunk! 1948, printed papers on card, 35.9 x 24.1 cm, Tate, London. © Trustees of the Paolozzi Foundation, Licensed by DACS, London 2018. 9cl. Rowntrees Fruit Gums, 1950s, photograph. Shawshots/Alamy. 9tr. Festival of Britain, 1951, photograph. National Archives/Getty Images. 10. Richard Hamilton, She, 1958-61, oil paint, cellulose nitrate paint, paper and plastic on wood, 121.9 x 81.3 cm, Tate, London. © The Estate of Richard Hamilton. All Rights Reserved. DACS, London 2018. 11. Peter Blake, On the Balcony, 1955-57, oil on canvas, 121.3 x 90.8 cm, Tate, London. © Peter Blake, All Rights Reserved. DACS, London 2018. 12. James Rosenquist, President Elect, 1960, oil on Masonite, 228 x 365.8 cm, Musêe d'Art Moderne, Paris. © James Rosenquist/DACS, London/VAGA, New York 2018. 13. John F Kennedy election poster, 1960, John F Kennedy Memorial Library & Museum, Boston, Ma. Richard Cummins/Superstock. 14. Wayne Thiebaud, Bakery Counter, 1962, oil on canvas, 139.4 x 182.6 cm, Private Collection. © Wayne Thiebaud/VAGA at ARS, NY and DACS, London 2018. Christies Images/Bridgeman Images. 15. Daniel Spoerri, Kichka's Breakfast, 1960, wooden chair hung on wall with board across seat, coffee pot, glass, bowls, egg cups, eggshell, cigarette butts, spoons, tin cans, 36.6 x 69.5x 65.4 cm, MOMA, New York. © Daniel Spoerri/ DACS, London 2018. Peter Horee/Alamy. 16. Claes Oldenburg, Floor Burger, 1962, canvas filled with foam rubber, cardboard boxes, painted with latex and Liquidtex, 1.32 x 2.13 m, Art Gallery of Ontario, Toronto. © Claes Oldenburg and Coosje van Bruggen. 17. Claes Oldenburg, Floor Cake, 1962, synthetic polymer paint and latex filled with foam rubber and cardboard boxes, 1.48 x 2.8 x 1.48 m, MOMA, New York. © Claes Oldenburg and Coosje van Bruggen. Rafa Rivas/AFP/Getty Images. 18. Andy Warhol, 32 Campbell's Soup Cans, 1962, synthetic polymer paint on thirty-two canvases, each canvas 50.8 x 40.6 cm, MOMA, New York. © 2018 The Andy Warhol Foundation for Visual Arts, Inc/Licensed by DACS, London. Peter Barritt/Superstock. 19. Andy Warhol in his studio, 1964, photograph. Mondadori/ Getty Images. 20. Tom Wesselmann, Landscape #4, 1965, acrylic and collage on fibreboard, Muzeum Ludwig, Budapest, Long-term loan from the Peter und Irene Ludwig Stiftung, Aachen. © Estate of Tom Wesselmann/DACS, London/VAGA, New York 2018. 21t. Allan D'Arcangelo. US Highway 1, 1963, acrylic on canvas, 121.9 x 139.7 cm, Smithsonian American Art Museum, Washington D.C. © Estate of Allan D'Arcangelo, DACS, London/VAGA, New York 2018. 21b. Ed Ruscha, Standard Station, 1966, screen print in colours on buff wove paper, 64.7 x 101.6 cm, Private Collection. ©Ed Ruscha. Christies Images/Bridgeman Images. 22. Roy Lichtenstein, In the Car,
1963, oil, Magna and graphite on canvas, 76.2 x 101.6 cm, Private Collection. © Estate of Roy Lichtenstein/DACS 2018. Christies Images/Superstock. 23t. Lichtenstein in his New York studio, 1968, photograph. Jack Mitchell/Getty Images. 23b. Roy Lichtenstein, Whaam! 1963, Magna acrylic and oil on canvas, 1.7 x 4m, Tate, London. © Estate of Roy Lichtenstein/DACS 2018. 24. Andy Warhol and members of the Velvet Underground, New York, 1966, photograph. Hervé Gloaguen/Gamma-Rapho via Getty Images. 25t. Peter Blake, Sergeant Pepper Lonely Hearts Club Band album cover, 1967. © Peter Blake. All Rights Reserved/DACS, London 2018. fototeca gilardi/Marka/Superstock. 25b. Mimmo Rotella, Elvis, 1964, torn posters on canvas, 197.7 x 137.8 cm. © Estate of Mimmo Rotella/DACS, London 2018. Christie's Images/Superstock. 26. Andy Warhol, Marilyn Diptych, 1962, acrylic paint on canvas, each 205.4 x 144.8 cm, Leo Castelli Gallery, New York. © 2018 The Andy Warhol Foundation for Visual Arts, Inc/Licensed by DACS, London. 4 x 5 Collection/Superstock. 27t. Allan D'Arcangelo, Marilyn, 1962, acrylic on canvas with string and scissors, 154.2 x 137.2 cm. Courtesy of Mitchell-Innes & Nash, N.Y.© Estate of Allan D'Arcangelo/DACS, London/VAGA, New York, 2018. 27b. Pauline Boty, The Only Blonde in the World, 1963, oil on canvas, 122.4 x 153 cm, Tate, London. © The Estate of Pauline Boty 2018. 28. Tom Wesselmann, Still Life # 30, 1963, oil, enamel and polymer paint on board with collage, plastic flowers and mixed media, 122 x 167.5 x 10 cm, MOMA, New York. © Estate of Tom Wesselmann/DACS, London/VAGA, NY 2018. 29. Roy Lichtenstein, Woman with Flowered Hat, 1963, Magna on canvas, 127.3 x 102.2 cm, Private Collection. © Estate of Roy Lichtenstein/DACS, London 2018. Peter Horee/Alamy. 30. Il Segno Art Gallery, photograph. Mario de Biasi/Mondadori via Getty Images. 31. Roy Lichtenstein, Turkey shopping bag, 1964, silkscreen on paper bag, 19.1 x 22.8 cm, MOMA, New York. © Estate of Roy Lichtenstein/DACS, London 2018. 32. George Segal, The Diner, c 1965, plaster, wood, chrome, laminated plastic, Masonite, fluorescent lamp, glass, paper, 238.76 x 366.40 x243.84 cm, Walker Art Center, Minneapolis. © The George and Helen Segal Foundation/VAGA, NY/DACS, London 2018. 33t. Model in studio of George Segal, 1977, photograph. Susan Wood/Getty Images. 33b. George Segal, Gay Liberation, bronze painted white, Stanford University Campus, permanent installation. Ken Wolter/Shutterstock. 34. James Rosenquist, F-111, 1964, oil on canvas with aluminium, 23 sections 304.8 x 2621.3 cm, MOMA, NY. © James Rosenquist/DACS, London/VAGA, New York 2018. Mario Tama/Getty Images. 35t. Robert Rauschenberg, Retroactive 1, 1963, oil and silkscreen ink on canvas, 213.4 x 152.4 cm, Wadsworth Atheneum, Hartford. © Robert Rauschenburg Foundation/DACS, London /VAGA, New York, 2018. 35b. Derek Boshier, I Wonder What My Heroes Think of the Space Race, 1962, oil on canvas, 241 x 174 cm, Government Art Collection. © Derek Boshier. All Rights Reserved, DACS, London 2018. Image Crown Copyright: UK Government Art Collection. 36. Pauline Boty, It's A Man's World 1, 1965, oil on canvas with collage. © The Estate of Pauline Boty 2018. Courtesy of Whitford Fine Art. 37t. Marisol in studio, 1964, photograph. CBS Photo Archive/Getty Images. 37b. Martha Rosler, Vacuuming Pop Art, from the series Body Beautiful or Beauty Knows no pain, c 1966-72. Photomontage. © Martha Rosler. Courtesy of the artist and Mitchell-Innes & Nash. 38. Robert Indiana, Love, 1967, screenprint on paper, 86.3 x 86.3 cm, Museum of Modern and Contemporary Art, Nice. © Morgan Art Foundation/ARS, New York and DACS London 2018. John Sohm/Alamy. 39. Robert Indiana, Love sculpture, Shinjuku, Tokyo, permanent installation. Christian Kober/Robert Harding PL. 40. David Hockney, A Bigger Splash, 1967, acrylic on canvas, 96 x 96 ", Tate, London. © David Hockney. © Tate, London 2018. 41. Patrick Caulfield, After Lunch, 1975, acrylic on canvas, 248.9 x 213.4 cm, Tate, London. © The Estate of Patrick Caulfield. All Rights Reserved, DACS, London 2018. 42. Öyvvind Fahlström, Column No 4, (IB Affair), 1974, silkscreen, 58.7 x 48.3 cm, MCA Chicago. © Estate of Ôyvind Fahlström/DACS, London 2018. 43t. Ushio Shinohara, Doll Festival, 1966, Triptych of screen prints on paper71.1 x 48.3 each, Hyogo Prefectural Museum of Art (Yamamura Collection. © Ushio + Noriko Shinohara. 43b. Alexander Kosolapov, Lenin and Coca Cola, 1982, proposed billboard for Times Square. © The artist/ ARS, NY and DACS, London, 2018. 44. Bridget Riley, Hesitate, 1964, emulsion on board, 106.7 x 110 cm, Tate London. © Bridget Riley 2018. © Tate, London 2018. All rights reserved. 45. Jeff Koons, Puppy, 1992. Stainless steel, soil and flowering plants, 1240 x 1240 x 820 cm. Guggenheim Museum, Bilbao. John Bower/Superstock. 46. Keith Haring, street art, Lower East Side, Manhattan, NY, graffiti. Patrice Hauser/Hemis/Superstock.

First published in Great Britain in 2018 by Wayland
Copyright © Hodder & Stoughton, 2018

All internet sites appearing in back matter were available and accurate when
this book was sent to press.

Printed and bound in China.
1593

Table of Contents

POP Goes the **Paint Pot!**   4

New Expressions   6

The **IG**   8

Pop Art Is   10

Pop **President**   12

Everything Is **beautiful**   14

Food on the Floor   16

The **Factory**   18

On the **Highway**   20

The Comic-Book **King**   22

Fame!   24

The Magic of **Marilyn**   26

Yesterday Today   28

The Great **Pop Shop**   30

Everyday People   32

War and **Space**   34

Girl-Power Pop   36

One **Small** Word   38

Anonymous **Worlds**   40

Popping the Globe   42

Pop **Lives** On   44

Glossary and **Read More**   46

Timeline   47

Index   48

POP Goes the Paint Pot!

Life is a little bit gray and gloomy . . . then POP, it fills with color and fun! That's what happened in the years following World War II (1939–45), when popular culture—and pop art—burst onto the scene.

What Is Pop Art?

Pop art was a movement that sprung up in the 1950s and 60s in the United Kingdom and the United States. These countries were fast recovering after the tough years of war. People had money to spend—and more things to spend it on as industry boomed. The pop artists saw fast cars, fast foods, TV, movies, and comic strips brightening up people's lives. They decided to use these to liven up the art world too!

Art for Everyone

Before pop, artists were exploring ways to depict their inner emotions, rather than what they saw in the physical world. The abstract expressionists painted plain blocks or splashes of color, which many people found hard to understand. The pop artists wanted *everyone* to understand their art! So they borrowed ideas from advertising, packaging, films, and magazines that people instantly recognized.

Bright advertising billboards light up 1960s New York.

Making It Modern

Pop brought art and life together into one kaleidoscopic world. Suddenly art galleries were full of soup cans, famous faces, cartoons, and giant lollipops! Techniques such as silk-screen printing, airbrushing, stenciling, and acrylic painting helped the images to look—or even be—mass-produced. Collage was another way of transferring everyday imagery into art, as you can see in Richard Hamilton's interior below.

Interior II, Richard Hamilton, 1964

Commercial Creators

In this new world of consumer products, art schools set up courses in commercial design. Many pop artists began as commercial artists. For example, in the United States, Andy Warhol designed shoes, Claes Oldenburg illustrated magazines, and James Rosenquist painted billboards. Other important pop artists included the Americans Roy Lichtenstein and Tom Wesselmann and the British artists Peter Blake and David Hockney.

New Expressions

In the decade before pop art emerged, there was a rollercoaster of change. During World War II, many artists fled from Europe to the United States, and New York took over from Paris as the center of the art world. It was here that the abstract expressionist style developed.

Abstract Feelings

Abstract expressionism was nonrepresentational—in other words, it wasn't meant to look like anything. Instead the artists tried to convey emotions, especially the trauma of war, which they felt representational art couldn't get across. Some painters, such as Mark Rothko, covered vast canvases with floating rectangles of color (right). Others, led by Jackson Pollock, flicked and dribbled paint in a method called action painting.

Untitled (Violet, Black, Orange, Yellow on White and Red), Mark Rothko, 1949

Look Closer

Rothko's paintings were often bigger than a person, with wide stripes of opposing colors. How does this one make you feel, and why?

Unemotional Art

In the early 1950s, artists including Robert Rauschenberg and Jasper Johns challenged the inwardness of abstract expressionism. They decided to make *un*emotional art using familiar, identifiable imagery. Rauschenberg created "Combines"—a mixture of painting and sculpture that incorporated everyday objects. Johns focused on "things which are seen and not looked at," such as flags, targets, and maps.

High-Brow, Low-Brow

This new approach became known as neo-Dada, for its similarity to a World War I movement called Dada. The Dadaists rebelled against tradition and invented "readymades"—ordinary objects, from bike wheels to urinals, that they signed as art. Images like Rauschenberg's *Bed* (right; made from his own pillow and quilt!) seemed to blur the same lines between high art and low culture. The seeds of American pop were sown.

"It is neither Art for Art, nor Art against Art. I am for Art, but for Art that has nothing to do with Art. Art has everything to do with life, but it has nothing to do with Art."
Robert Rauschenberg

Bed, Robert Rauschenberg, 1955

Looking Back

Pop art drew from other past styles too. Around 1911 the cubists Pablo Picasso and Georges Braque introduced lettering, collage, and found objects into their work. Then in the 1920s, surrealists including Salvador Dalí and René Magritte developed a dream-world style. They combined unlikely images, such as a lobster and a telephone, which brought a new wit to art. This tongue-in-cheek humor soon found its way into pop art.

The IG

In 1952 a group of young artists in London began meeting at the new Institute of Contemporary Arts. They called themselves the Independent Group, or IG, and they got together to shake up what they saw to be an elitist art world.

Group Discussions

The IG artists included Richard Hamilton and Eduardo Paolozzi. Along with other artists, architects, and critics, they talked (and argued!) about modern life, technology, fame, science fiction . . . and the place of mass culture in fine art. At the first meeting, Paolozzi gave a lecture called "Bunk!" (nonsense), based on collages that he had made from magazine clippings, postcards, and other commercial snippets.

Meet the People, one of the collages from "Bunk!," Eduardo Paolozzi, 1948

Look Closer

Paolozzi's collages, which he made in a scrapbook, are sometimes called the first pop art. Can you see similarities between this and the ad on page 9?

Awesome America

The material that Paolozzi used in his collages was all-American, collected from U.S. soldiers stationed in Europe after the war. Britain in the early 1950s was still rebuilding its war-torn cities. Though events like the Festival of Britain (1951) and the coronation of Queen Elizabeth II (1953) filled people with national pride, there was a fascination with the rich and glamorous world that American culture seemed to offer.

The Festival of Britain on London's South Bank, 1951

Ads in the 1950s were bright, bold, and direct.

Consumer Imagery

For the first time, Britain was importing American TV, fast food outlets, and other consumer products. Rock and blues music and Hollywood stars were taking the world by storm. As big names and brands competed, advertising became more important and new efforts went into packaging design. The IG recognized that this commercial imagery was less intimidating to ordinary people than traditional gallery art.

This Is Tomorrow

The IG published articles and staged exhibitions, including the groundbreaking *This is Tomorrow* in 1956. This was a collaborative event with a jukebox playing and a wide range of work. It presented art as entertainment, with a sense of fun and optimism that serious wartime painting and sculpture lacked. The IG were making art in a new context—the good times.

"We felt none of the dislike of commercial culture standard among most intellectuals, but accepted it as fact. . . . One result . . . was to take pop culture out of the realm of escapism, entertainment, and relaxation, and treat it with the seriousness of art."

Lawrence Alloway, writer and IG member

Pop Art Is

In 1957 Richard Hamilton wrote a letter to two architects from the IG, listing the "characteristics of Pop Art." He was describing images designed to appeal to the masses—not the kind of art usually seen in galleries.

A Famous Quote
This is what Hamilton wrote:

> Pop Art is:
> Popular (designed for a mass audience)
> Transient (short-term solution)
> Expendable (easily forgotten)
> Low cost
> Mass-produced
> Young (aimed at youth)
> Witty
> Sexy
> Gimmicky
> Glamorous
> Big business

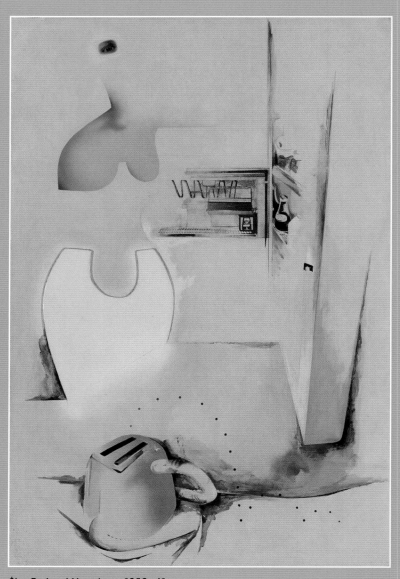

$he, Richard Hamilton, 1958–61

Art as Commentary
Hamilton wasn't talking about pop art as we know it today, but he was observing how certain types of art can both grab attention and manipulate people's lives. He explored this idea in his work. For example, in *$he* (above) he painted part of a female figure beside an image of an oven and a toaster. It was a comment on the way ads for household products often used attractive women to help them sell.

British vs. American Pop

British pop often quietly criticized or parodied consumer culture as well as celebrating it. It was usually less brash than U.S. pop, which reveled in loud, commercial images as a contrast to abstract expressionism. While many American pop artists used modern techniques such as silk-screen printing and airbrushing, the British tended to be more traditional with their painting and collage.

On the Balcony, Peter Blake, 1955–57

Blake's Balcony

Peter Blake was an important British pop artist who met Hamilton at the Royal College of Art in London. His *On the Balcony* (above) is an oil painting that looks at culture old and new. It includes 27 variations on the balcony theme, from a 19th-century painting by Édouard Manet to a photo of the British royal family. There are also plenty of everyday features—magazines, pin buttons, and a group of grumpy teenagers!

Pop President

What do a U.S. president, a chocolate cake, and a comfortable car have in common? They're all manufactured to attract the consumer—or so this painting by James Rosenquist seems to say!

President Elect, James Rosenquist, 1960–61

Advertising Image

Rosenquist painted president-elect John F. Kennedy (above) as though he was a product being advertised. In fact, JFK had been advertising himself, making full use of the mass media in his campaign to be elected that year. The face in this painting came from one of his campaign posters (right). Rosenquist used it along with magazine clippings to make a small source collage. Then he drew a grid on the collage and scaled it up to create his enormous painting.

Mixed Message

Rosenquist loved to combine fragmented images, like the flashes of things we see out of the corner of our eye. He often used a mixture of bright color and monochrome, and put together unlikely objects just as the surrealists had done decades before. Although the parts of this painting seem unconnected, they were a sharp observation of culture at the time. "Buy to improve your life!" was the general message.

Hands-free Style

The lines on the painting look just like the joins on a billboard. Rosenquist trained as a sign painter, and he worked hard to recreate the same smooth, glossy style. He drew and painted freehand, without any help from image-editing software. (It didn't exist back then!) By avoiding visible brushstrokes, he made his pictures look anonymous, as if no artist's hand were involved.

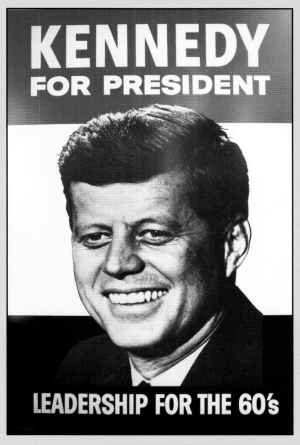

A Kennedy campaign poster from 1960

·▶ Look Closer

Rosenquist painted this in oils with ordinary brushes (in later work he also used an airbrush). Notice how he blended the different images together. Do you think the picture would have a different impact if it were all in color, or all black and white?

Assassination

JFK was the ultimate pop president—handsome, youthful, and media-savvy. He also hit the headlines tragically in 1963, when he was assassinated by a gunman. Several pop artists, including Andy Warhol, created work in response to the attack. Robert Rauschenberg, who had already begun making his piece *Retroactive I* (see page 35), decided to keep JFK's image in it to honor his memory.

Everything Is Beautiful

In May 1962, *Time* magazine ran an article called "The Slice of Cake School." It featured several American artists—including Andy Warhol, Wayne Thiebaud, and Roy Lichtenstein—who all seemed to share a fascination with food!

Bakery Counter, Wayne Thiebaud, 1962

Look Closer

Most pop artists painted or printed in flat colors with little shading. Wayne Thiebaud used thick paint, or impasto, on these cakes. What effect does it have?

Making a Movement

While the British pop artists were already an established group by the late 1950s, the movement arose differently in the United States. Most of the British artists either taught or studied at the Royal Academy of Art in London, but the American artists worked in isolation from one another. It was only in the early 1960s that common themes (including cake!) began identifying them as the core of U.S. pop.

New Exhibitions

In the autumn of 1962, an exhibition called *The New Realists* took place in New York. This united Warhol, Lichtenstein, Rosenquist, Oldenburg, and others with like-minded artists from Europe. Many of the European artists, such as Yves Klein and Jean Tinguely, were already well established and helped to attract attention. A similarly important show, *The New Painting of Common Objects*, was held in Pasadena, California, the same year.

Everyday Icons

Pop art features such as bright colors, popular imagery, and commercial styles were starting to emerge as a trend. Pop artists were reinventing everyday things as icons of the modern times. Warhol later declared, "Everything is beautiful. Pop is everything." Why shouldn't a cake or a car be art as long as people wanted to look at it!

Kichka's Breakfast, Daniel Spoerri, 1960

Nouveau Réalisme

The concept of beauty in everything was flourishing in Europe too. The nouveaux réalistes (new realists), as the group in Paris was known, included a French artist called Arman who made box sculptures filled with mass-produced items or even trash. Meanwhile, the Swiss Daniel Spoerri—who took part in the 1962 New York show—"trapped" the remains of meals and other things by fixing them to the table surface and then hanging the whole thing on a wall (above)!

Food on the Floor

A giant, soft hamburger, slumped on a gallery floor—should you touch it, sit on it, or just look at it? You certainly wouldn't want to eat it—Claes Oldenburg made it out of painted canvas stuffed with plastic foam and cardboard boxes!

Floor Burger, Claes Oldenburg, 1962

Sloppy Surprise

Oldenburg built the enormous burger—it measured 4 feet 4 inches by 7 feet (1.32 by 2.13 meters)—with the help of his wife, Pat Muchinski, a skilled seamstress. To avoid having to transport it afterward, they made it inside the gallery in Manhattan, New York. The finished work was deliberately imperfect—it was roughly painted and looked, according to one visitor, a bit "sloppy." People in 1962 had never seen anything like it before!

The Store

Oldenburg was no stranger to food sculpture. In 1961 he had opened up a shop in Manhattan called The Store. Here he sold small pieces made of painted plaster, including ice cream cones, underwear, rib eye steak, and blueberry pie. He even had a mock plaster cash register! People could buy what he called "ham art, pork art, chicken art, tomato art, banana art, apple art, turkey art, cake art . . ." while out doing their everyday shopping.

Big Softies

Manhattan was an area where huge grand pianos and luxury cars were displayed in indoor showrooms. Oldenburg decided to upscale his work and present larger-than-life sculptures in the same way! Alongside his burger, he exhibited a massive *Floor Cake* (below) and *Floor Cone*. By making all these giants soft, he broke the tradition of sculpture being solid and inflexible.

Saucy Protest

Oldenburg's work is full of humor and fun, both saluting and laughing at American culture. But not everyone appreciated his work at first. When the Art Gallery of Ontario purchased *Floor Burger* in 1967, local students and teachers protested with an oversized plywood ketchup bottle! Oldenburg didn't care—he simply said, "They should have made it out of something soft."

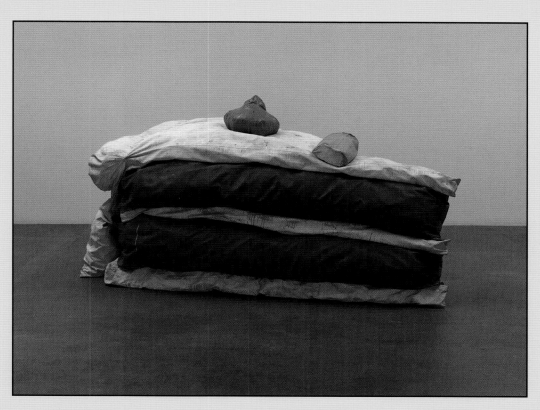

Claes Oldenburg's *Floor Cake* (1962), on display at the Guggenheim Bilbao Museum in Spain

"We don't copy the objects we use, we try to transform them and we hope they go on transforming as you look at them."
Claes Oldenburg

The Factory

Art is precious. Art is unique. Art is one-off, original, and lovingly handcrafted . . . or is it? Andy Warhol turned these ideas on their head when he ran his studio like a factory!

Multiple Impact

Warhol believed that similar or identical copies of a work should be just as valuable as the original. To him, the impact of the art itself was far more important than the making of it. So when Warhol found an image that he liked, he repeated it! He used a method called silk-screen printing to create multiple pictures of soup cans, cola bottles, dollar bills, celebrities, and more.

32 Campbell's Soup Cans, Andy Warhol, 1962

Look Closer

Warhol mimicked the design of Campbell's soup cans and made them in every flavor (above). In what ways do you think his prints differ from advertising images? How are they the same?

The Printing Process

Screen printing was a commercial process that appealed to Warhol for its machinelike results. It involved transferring an image onto a fine mesh screen and blocking certain areas like a stencil. Then the screen would be placed over a canvas before dragging ink or paint across it with a rubber squeegee. This forced the ink or paint through unblocked parts of the screen onto the canvas.

Andy Warhol in his studio in 1964. Many of the prints show the famous face of Jacqueline Kennedy, John F. Kennedy's widow.

Production Line

Warhol called his studio "The Factory" and set it up for mass production. He employed assistants to help make his screen prints, though the original designs were always his own. Warhol's art was printed on big canvases, small canvases, shopping bags, and other objects, and usually sold as limited editions (a set number of works). Occasionally an assistant would even sign for Warhol—he was happy with that!

Art or Advertising?

Some critics criticized Warhol's mass-market approach and the way he replicated popular imagery. Surely this was just another form of advertising—there was no longer any distance between art and its source. But Warhol was promoting brands and faces that everyone recognized, and in turn this helped him to sell his work. He was reaching a wider audience by making art less exclusive and by making it quickly.

"The reason I'm painting this way is that I want to be a machine, and I feel that whatever I do and do machine-like is what I want to do."

Andy Warhol

19

On the Highway

Shiny cars on the open road, streetlights, gas stations, bright neon signs . . . the 1950s and 60s were boom times for the U.S. motor industry, and pop artists were quick to jump aboard.

Speedy Symbols

In a world where war was still a recent memory, cars were a symbol of freedom and adventure. American car production was at an all-time high, and people were driving bigger, faster, more stylish vehicles. Billboards were plastered with car ads showing exciting new features, from space-age tail fins to chrome detailing. Artists captured their glossy, thrilling feel in paintings like Tom Wesselmann's below.

Landscape #4, Tom Wesselmann, 1965

Changing Landscape

The culture of the car soon changed the landscape of the United States. From 1956 the Interstate Highway System greatly expanded the road network so that people could travel farther in less time. New businesses sprang up, from motels and gas stations to drive-in movies and restaurants. All this inspired pop work.

The Endless Road

D'Arcangelo's painting (right) shows one of the older U.S. highways—Route 1, on the East Coast. Perhaps he painted it with a sense of nostalgia as the interstate system was developing. It certainly has a dreamlike feel, with the empty road and floating signs. It's as if we're in a car, on a very long trip, staring hypnotically ahead as things flicker into our vision. D'Arcangelo used quick-drying acrylic paint, another product of the 1950s, to help him create crisp edges.

US Highway 1, Allan D'Arcangelo, 1963

Standard Station, Ed Ruscha, 1966

Landmarks and Trademarks

Ed Ruscha saw plenty of Standard gas stations on his journeys across the U.S. He wanted to make them seem monumental, so he showed this one above looming in a bright, dynamic sweep against the sky. The brand name "Standard" was interesting to Ruscha because it had many possible meanings. He was often inspired by typography and trademarks in his work.

Mixed Interpretations

Other artists had their own ways of immortalizing the highway. Andy Warhol silk-screened multiple images of a fatal car accident. Billy Al Bengston created art with automotive paint—the same stuff that decorated the motorcycles he raced! In France, the new realist César made sculptures from compressed vehicles, having watched them being crushed at a scrapyard.

21

The Comic-Book King

In the highly competitive world of pop, it was important for artists to stand out. Who could do what first, and how? Roy Lichtenstein carved his niche as the king of comic-style painting.

Cool Cartoons

Comic books became popular in the 1930s, when characters like Superman were born. Lichtenstein grew up to love the drama and energy of comics. He was fascinated by the way they conveyed intense emotion in a cool, mechanical style. The stories and characters seemed larger than life—so Lichtenstein recreated them that way!

In the Car, Roy Lichtenstein, 1963

Look Closer

This painting is over six and a half feet (two m) long in real life! How can we tell the car is moving? How has Lichtenstein made the scene seem tense?

Single Scenes

Lichtenstein scoured comic strips for individual scenes that inspired him, then he turned these into massive paintings. Often he included thought bubbles or speech bubbles and focused on theatrical close-ups. Showing a single frame from a story created a sense of mystery that challenged viewers to fill in the gaps. Where are these people in the car above going, for example, and what are they talking about?

Lots of Dots

Comics were printed using a process called Ben-Day dots in four colors—cyan, magenta, yellow, and black. Lichtenstein used perforated stencils to help him mimic the dots, only his were bigger. He used the same four colors and heavy outlines, working with oil or acrylic paints. Sometimes he copied comics almost exactly; at other times he altered things, such as the type and number of planes shown in *Whaam!* (below).

Lichtenstein in his New York studio, 1968

Whaam! Roy Lichtenstein, 1963

Expensive Copies

Lichtenstein was often criticized for his copying—after all, he was turning cheap, throw-away images into valuable works of art. How would the comic-book artists feel about this? *Whaam!* (above), for example, was based on an issue of *All-American Men of War*, but the man who drew the original story did not become famous or make a lot of money.

Fame!

There was no such thing as YouTube, social networking, or reality TV in the 1960s. But Warhol still predicted, "In the future, everyone in the world will be famous for 15 minutes." Fame was a big thing for the pop artists—they wanted it, and they painted it!

All-Star Moment

This was a time when the world was churning out stars—musicians from the Beatles to Elvis Presley; actors from John Wayne to Marilyn Monroe. They were unmistakable icons, getting noticed in glossy magazines, movies, and on a growing number of household TVs. And just like Campbell's soup, pop art only added to their fame!

Warhol with members of the band The Velvet Underground

Pop Publicity

The pop artists worked in all sorts of media. Warhol, in particular, saw that there were many possible routes to fame. He wrote books, made films, and even briefly managed a rock band, The Velvet Underground (above). Other artists held lectures or appeared in documentaries, such as *Pop Goes the Easel* in Britain. Pop soon started to influence commercial design and fashions, and so its familiarity spread more.

Celebrity Cover

The relationship between stars and their fans particularly interested Peter Blake. In addition to fine art, he created album covers, including the Beatles' *Sergeant Pepper's Lonely Hearts Club Band* (right). For this he and his wife made cutouts of famous people, which were then photographed together with the real Beatles (and wax dummies of them!).

Sergeant Pepper's Lonely Hearts Club Band album cover, Peter Blake and Jann Haworth, 1967

Elvis Presley, Mimmo Rotella, 1964

Off the Wall

Mimmo Rotella was an Italian artist who used film posters as his starting point. Instead of making collages, he created the opposite—décollages (left). Collecting torn posters from the walls of Rome, he started gluing them onto canvas and peeling pieces off. Often he did this in layers, revealing parts of different posters with every tear.

The Magic of Marilyn

Of all the stars of stage or screen, Marilyn Monroe made the biggest pop! She was irresistible to artists on both sides of the Atlantic, and they celebrated her image in many different forms.

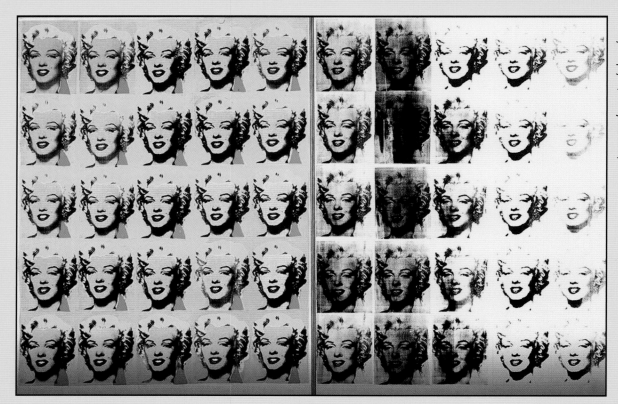

Marilyn Diptych, Andy Warhol, 1962

Eternal Icon

Marilyn was an American actor, model, and singer, renowned for her "blonde bombshell" looks. She was iconic in her lifetime, but her early death in 1962 shocked the world and shot her to even greater fame. Almost immediately after she died, Warhol honored her in a double silk screen, *Marilyn Diptych* (above). He based it on a 1953 publicity photograph and showed her face fifty times, half in color and half in fading black-and-white.

Look Closer

A diptych is an image created in two parts. Why do you think Warhol chose to depict Marilyn in this way? What themes does he address on each side of the diptych?

Person or Doll?

James Rosenquist and Allan D'Arcangelo were also quick to commemorate Marilyn. D'Arcangelo was angry about the way the media had treated her as a symbol more than a person. He painted her as a paper doll with her features to one side, ready to be cut out and slotted in (right). This suggests that she was fragile and manipulated, but when you put the pieces back together, her image will always be the same.

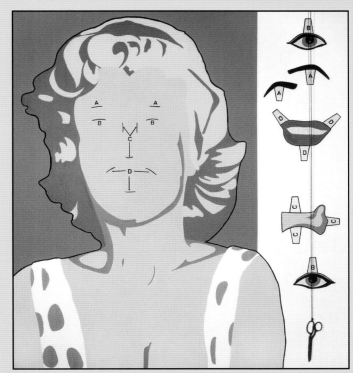

Marilyn, Allan D'Arcangelo, 1962

Checks and Crosses

A few months after Marilyn's death, the British magazine *Town* featured a full spread of photos of her. She had always insisted on vetting images before publishing, and these ones were annotated with her own checks and cross-outs. Two years later, Richard Hamilton photographed the article and used the pictures to create a collage. He highlighted her exact marks by painting over them in oils.

The Only Blonde in the World, Pauline Boty, 1963

Honored by All

Almost every other pop artist has a Marilyn image to show. Before she died, Peter Blake made a Marilyn door and Peter Philips, a collage. Tom Wesselmann painted her mouth, Roy Lichtenstein showed her in dots, and for Pauline Boty she was *The Only Blonde in the World* (left). In 1967 the Sidney Janis Gallery in New York held an *Homage to Marilyn Monroe* exhibition, featuring the above artists plus Oldenburg, Rauschenberg, Paolozzi, Arman, Rotella, and many more.

Yesterday Today

**The British artist Pauline Boty called pop "a nostalgia for now."
It very much was in its obsession with contemporary times—
but pop also looked back to the past.**

Traditional Subjects

The pop artists were very conscious of previous trends in art and looked for ways to connect them to the present. Traditional subjects, such as nudes, landscapes, and interiors, were taken up in a new way. Sodas and fast foods were really just modern interpretations of the old-fashioned still life. Portraits of Marilyn or Elvis were still portraits, even if they weren't painted formally.

Kitchen Collage

Tom Wesselmann was one artist who embraced the tradition of still life and brought it right up to date. He used a combination of paint (including acrylic and enamel), collage, and real 3-D objects in his bright, mixed-media work. For this image below, he stuck on a pink fridge door, plastic flowers, and plastic replicas of 7UP bottles. He also cut out pictures from printed ads and incorporated them into his huge artwork.

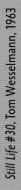

Still Life #30, Tom Wesselmann, 1963

Look Closer

Wesselmann's still lifes reflected popular products of the time. Do you recognize some of them? What would you include in a collage to sum up everyday life today? How would you make it? What materials would you use?

Dotty Masters

Although Roy Lichtenstein is most famous for his comic pictures, he used the same style to emulate some of the great masters of art. He searched museums for paintings to transform, paying homage to Claude Monet, Pablo Picasso, Salvador Dalí, and many others. In a sense he was making their work his own, like this interpretation of a Picasso (below). Perhaps he was also commenting on the way popular art was reprinted on postcards, calendars, and so on.

Woman with Flowered Hat, Roy Lichtenstein, 1963

Nostalgic Memories

For some pop artists, looking backward meant exploring childhood memories. Peter Blake, for example, made a toy shop assemblage, while Warhol's *Toy Paintings* were based on toys and books that he had collected over the years. Jim Dine recreated a child's bedroom wall, starry blue and lit by an actual lamp. Other artists looked at old film or comic characters, such as American Mel Ramos and his *Man of Steel*, a 1930s Superman.

The Great Pop Shop

As if pop needed any more attention, some landmark exhibitions in the mid-1960s provided it. The U.S. art market had already warmed to the style—but there were still a few surprises!

The American Supermarket

In 1964 a small space on the Upper East Side of Manhattan was transformed by a group of pop artists into *The American Supermarket*. It looked just like a self-service food store, which fooled some shoppers into thinking they could buy genuine groceries! In fact, they weren't far off—as part of the exhibit, Andy Warhol had signed a collection of real soup cans and was selling them for $6.50 each.

Notable Events

Six Painters and the Object took place in 1963 at the Guggenheim Museum in New York. This high-profile venue, relocated in 1959 to Frank Lloyd Wright's iconic building, was acknowledgment in itself that pop was by now considered worthy art. In 1964, Robert Rauschenberg was awarded the grand prize for his silk screens at the prestigious Venice Biennale in Italy. It was a controversial win, but one that shifted the world's gaze in pop's direction.

A reconstruction of *The American Supermarket*, with Warhol's *Brillo Boxes* and Lichtenstein's shopping bags

Inedible Groceries

The American Supermarket opened for four weeks, with music playing inside and a real hot-dog stand outside. The gallery owners wore ribboned boater hats and took orders on grocer's pads. Among the products on sale were candies by Oldenburg, a giant plastic turkey by Wesselmann, chrome and felt eggs by Robert Watts, Andy Warhol's *Brillo Boxes,* and some very heavy bronze ale cans by Jasper Johns. Images by Warhol and Lichtenstein were silk-screened onto shopping bags and snapped up for a few dollars each.

Turkey Shopping Bag, Roy Lichtenstein, 1964

"Lock up a department store today, open the door after a hundred years, and you will have a museum of art."
Andy Warhol

Art in Life

The ultimate merging of art and life happened at *The American Supermarket*. People walked around town with the shopping bags, making use of them in the outside world. The exhibition raised more questions about "appropriation," or the borrowing of pre-existing images to make art. Warhol's signed soup cans were 30 times more expensive than the unsigned versions—and they would cost a lot more now!

Everyday People

A bright-white man sits at a counter while a bright-white woman makes him coffee. He'll be waiting a long time because both figures are made of plaster! They are the work of American pop sculptor George Segal.

The Consumer

While other pop artists focused on consumables—foods,, brand names, cars—Segal did the reverse. He looked at the consumer—the ordinary human swept up in the deluge of mass marketing and mass production. While other pop artists were bright, bold, loud, and unmissable, Segal's work was understated and calm.

Anonymous Moment

In an ironic way, instead of consuming, these two figures (at right) seem almost consumed by their environment. While everything around them is real and in color, they are not. They are anonymous and silent, frozen in an undefined moment. The garish red wall demands more attention than they do.

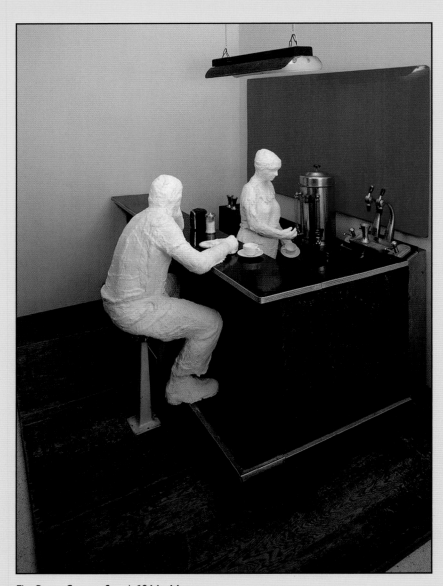

The Diner, George Segal, 1964–66

Look Closer

Segal very rarely added color to his figures. Why do you think he preferred to keep them plain white? What sort of feelings do they conjure up?

Bandaged Up

To create his sculptures, Segal used orthopedic bandages dipped in plaster. He would borrow people—usually family or friends; sometimes himself—and cover them in the bandages to make a cast. When the plaster hardened, he carefully cut it off and reassembled it. The result was a hollow, rough-surfaced, life-size replica of a person.

A model being cast in George Segal's studio

Segal's *Gay Liberation* monument at Stanford University, California

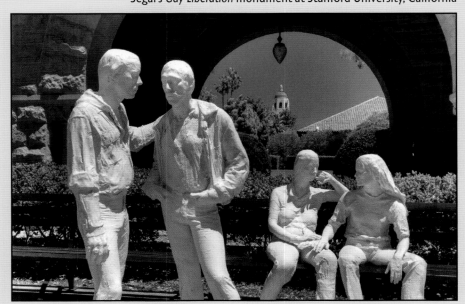

In the Real World

Segal placed his figures in everyday settings. One sat at a table, one stood in a bath, another rode a bicycle, and so on. Later Segal began putting the figures in public places so that people could walk around them and interact with them. At this stage he had the plaster models cast in bronze to make them tougher—but he usually still painted them white.

"My biggest job is to select and freeze the gestures that are most telling . . ."
George Segal

War and Space

For all its celebration of desirable products and people, pop had a dark side too. The world was feeling tension between the United States and the Soviet Union as they competed to be the greatest superpower. Pop artists responded to the global news through their work.

The Cold War

After World War II, the United States and Soviet Union were the world's most powerful nations. Neither wanted the other to gain more power, and their rivalry became known as the Cold War. Although they never fought directly, they backed their allies in proxy wars, including the Vietnam War (1955–1975), and both sides openly tested nuclear weapons.

Hope and Fear

American pop artists noticed contradictions between their country's great prosperity and its potential to end the world. Just as new technologies improved people's lives, they could also be used catastrophically. James Rosenquist captured this feeling in a gigantic panoramic image painted during the Vietnam War (below). It shows a U.S. fighter-bomber weaving through snapshots of both hopeful and fearful America.

The full extent of *F-111* by James Rosenquist, 1964–65

Look Closer

Rosenquist's painting was designed to surround all four walls of a room. It includes a smiling child under a missilelike hairdryer and a beach umbrella being blasted by a nuclear bomb. What else can you see? Why do you think Rosenquist included these images?

The Space Race

Competition between the United States and the Soviet Union didn't end with weapons and power. It also launched the Space Race—a fight to be the best at space technology. After the Soviets put the first manned spacecraft in orbit, President Kennedy declared that an American would be the first to walk on the moon. He died before his dream came true, but Robert Rauschenberg showed the president alongside an astronaut in this screen print (right) that looks like a mash-up of news reports.

Retroactive I, Robert Rauschenburg, 1963

I Wonder What My Heroes Think of the Space Race, Derek Boshier, 1962

In Other News . . .

Other pop artists, including the British Derek Boshier, painted the thrill of the Space Race (left). Meanwhile Gerald Laing and Pauline Boty, also British, responded to the Cuban Missile Crisis of 1962, arguably the closest the world has come to nuclear war. Warhol captured the notorious race riots in Alabama in 1963, as supporters of the U.S. civil rights movement fought for racial equality. And the Icelandic artist Erró turned the tables on the Vietnam War, painting Viet Cong freedom fighters invading comfortable U.S. homes.

"The artist's job is to be a witness to his time in history."
Robert Rauschenberg

Girl-Power Pop

Pop, like most previous art movements, was predominantly a boys' club. The male artists attracted the most attention. But there were also many important female artists, who are now better recognized for their work.

It's a Man's World I, Pauline Boty, 1965

Female Empowerment

The male pop artists often portrayed women as targets of attraction. Many female artists responded to this by focusing on female empowerment. Sometimes they mocked men's attitudes toward women or addressed the way they were the forgotten gender in art. Evelyne Axell, Marjorie Strider, Rosalyn Drexler, and Chryssa were just a few examples of women who proved their pop worth.

Boty Goes Pop

Pauline Boty was a leading figure in British pop, a bit of a rebel and a star in *Pop Goes the Easel*. She died very young with her art fairly unknown, but she is now praised for her revolutionary feminism. Boty's work was passionate, unlike the more detached male pop, and often criticized the "man's world" she lived in. The collage above shows a rose as a symbol of women, blooming among glorified men.

Boxy Star

The French-Venezuelan Marisol (Escobar) went only by her first name. Sometimes artists did this to hide the fact that they were women, but Marisol was proud of her gender. Her work had a level of emotion that separated her from mainstream pop. She made playful boxy sculptures (right) of film stars, presidents, and other icons, as well as her own family.

Marisol posing with some of her sculptures on a TV documentary in 1964

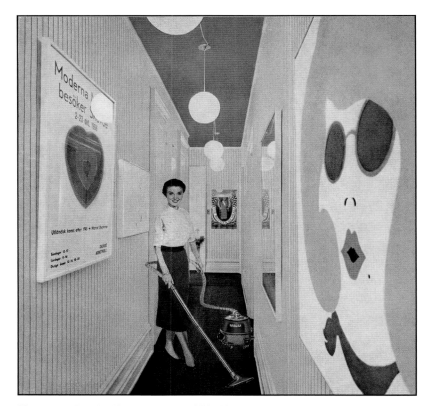

Vacuuming Pop Art, Martha Rosler, 1966–72

Vacuuming Pop Art

American Martha Rosler's photomontage *Vacuuming Pop Art* (left) looks like a typical domestic ad. But this is a witty comment on expected roles and the way women in pop art were sidelined. A well-groomed woman is happily cleaning—or perhaps she is just resigned to it. The hall she is vacuuming is decorated with well-known works, including one of a glamorous woman, by male pop artists.

In Focus: One **Small** Word

In 1965 Robert Indiana created a Christmas card for the Museum of Modern Art in New York. He used nothing more than the letters of the word LOVE, but the world fell head over heels for his design.

Signs and Symbols

Indiana was always interested in signage, stenciling, and the power of ordinary words. He liked crisp edges, clean colors, circles, and other geometric shapes. He was inspired by images of the U.S., from pinball machines to highway signs. The original idea for using the word *love* came from a "God is Love" inscription on the Christian Science church he went to as a child.

LOVE, Robert Indiana, 1967

Letters of Love

Can a simple word be art? Indiana made it happen! He tilted the O so it seems to swoon and chose a warm, bright red, the color of love. The word is enclosed in a neat quartered square, as if being given a hug. It quickly became an emblem of the hippy "love generation" and later appeared on a best-selling U.S. postage stamp.

Copies and Critics

Unfortunately Indiana failed to copyright his design, and because it was a simple word, people copied it without permission. Cheap knockoffs were rushed out on everything from T-shirts to beer mugs. Indiana was accused of being a sellout and pandering to popular tastes, whereas the truth was he was making no money from the unauthorized reproductions.

Robert Indiana's *LOVE* sculpture in Tokyo, Japan

Sharing the Love

Indiana did recreate *LOVE* himself in a variety of colors, compositions, and materials. In 1970 he made his first major *LOVE* sculpture, a huge monument in plain steel. First displayed in the Indianapolis Museum of Art, there are now versions of it all around the world (above), including ones in Spanish and Hebrew. In 2008, Indiana designed *Hope* for the Barack Obama presidential election campaign, and in 2011 a Valentine's Google Doodle appeared in his famous style!

"In our culture we have words—marks the typewriter makes—and they're not very attractive, are they? It's the role of the artist—my particular role, if you will—to make words and numbers very, very special."

Robert Indiana

Anonymous Worlds

Two British pop artists from Peter Blake's generation made some of their best-known work in the late 1960s and 70s. David Hockney and Patrick Caulfield painted enigmatic worlds in very individual styles.

Own Directions

Hockney, Caulfield, and Blake all met while studying at London's Royal College of Art. They shared an interest in painting the everyday, but they each took this in their own direction. Caulfield was less focused on popular culture than rekindling traditional subjects with commercial materials and techniques. Hockney turned to modern acrylic paints and a detached style to create his famous poolside scenes.

A Bigger Splash, David Hockney, 1967

Painting Pools

Hockney quickly made a name for himself as a leading artist in the U.K. In 1964 he visited California where he subsequently settled for many years. He was struck by the number of swimming pools in Los Angeles, which had a much sunnier climate than his native Britain. They were essentially an everyday feature there, and he painted them repeatedly.

40

A Slow Splash

A Bigger Splash (far left) is mysterious in that there's a hint, but no sight, of a person. Everything is anonymous, quiet, and still ... except for the big splash in the pool. Hockney spent two weeks painting that splash! He was amused that he could take an instantaneous moment and act it out in slow motion using fine lines, stipples, and dribbles. To achieve the posterlike effect in the rest of the image, he applied his paint with a roller.

After Lunch, Patrick Caulfield, 1975

Inside Outlines

Caulfield also laid his paint down very evenly in the bright blue scene above. A stripe of paler blue suggests a shaft of light across the room, but most of the image is in outline. The only thing painted realistically is the unreal picture (copied from a photographic poster) on the wall. A fish tank in front of it brings the water from the picture into the room. Meanwhile a waiter leans quietly in the corner. Are we meant to notice him at all?

Look Closer ◄·········

Caulfield made a familiar setting look strange and mysterious. What do the black outlines remind you of? Why do you think he chose blue for his main color? What different moods would other colors create?

41

Popping the Globe

It soon became apparent that the world had gone pop—not just the U.K. and U.S. The big exhibitions of the early to mid-1960s had a global impact, and parallel movements sprung up in countries far and wide.

A World of Approaches

Pop had offshoots all around Europe, as well as in Latin America, Asia, and the Middle East. In each case, the style was rooted in popular culture, the mass media, and modern techniques. But individual countries explored their own points of view, based on their local traditions and society. Sometimes they challenged the dominance of the United States and the way its products were infiltrating the world.

Column no. 4 (IB affair), Öyvind Fahlström, 1974

European Realism

New realism was one of the first partners to pop, based in Paris, France. Meanwhile in Germany it took the form of capitalist realism, with artists including Gerhard Richter, Wolf Vostell, and Sigmar Polke. Like the original pop artists, they focused on consumerism and the popular press, as well as a fascination with the United States. Often their art was political—as was the work of Swedish Öyvind Fahlström, who drew in a busy cartoon style (left).

Tokyo Pop

Japan was occupied by the United States for seven years after World War II. The country was saturated with American culture, but its artists did more than just copy pop. They looked to their own customs and mixed them with commercial approaches. Ushio Shinohara, for example, painted Japanese women in traditional costume, using graphic shapes and fluorescent colors (below). He is still making work in a new signature style—punching his canvas with boxing gloves dipped in paint!

Doll Festival, Ushio Shinohara, 1966

Communist Pop

For communist countries where art was monitored, pop came later in the 1970s and 80s. The everyday in the Soviet Union and China was more about glorious leaders and party propaganda than soda and mass-production, though Alexander Kosolapov combined both in his *Lenin and Coca Cola* (right). Leonid Sokov likewise put together a dictator and a Western idol in his *Two Profiles (Stalin and Marilyn).* In China, political pop took a similarly ironic view.

Kosolapov's *Lenin and Coca Cola* in Times Square, New York, 1982

Pop Lives On

In 1968, Andy Warhol was shot and injured by a radical women's rights activist and never fully recovered. Many people see this as the beginning of the end for pop art. Although other styles of art began to compete, pop left an unforgettable mark.

New Directions

As the 1960s came to an end, artists started to question where else pop could go. It was time to find new ways to blur lines between art and life. From around 1964, op artists like Bridget Riley captured the dazzle of modern society with abstract, eye-boggling patterns (right). Then photorealists like Richard Estes developed a style so convincing that their paintings could be everyday snapshots.

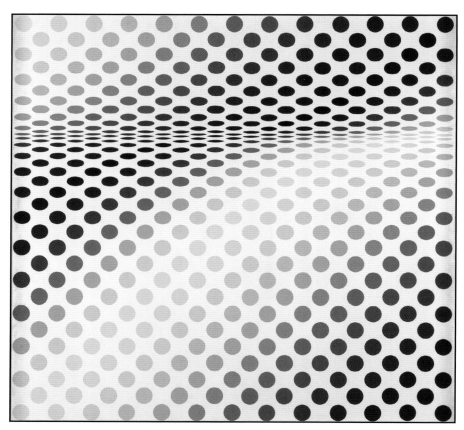

Hesitate, Bridget Riley, 1964

Continued Work

Styles such as land art, feminist art, and performance art followed, but nonetheless pop artists kept working. Warhol enjoyed renewed success with his silk screens in the 1980s, Hockney began making "joiners" or photomontages, and Oldenburg and his wife went even bigger with their sculptures—a giant saw, clothespin, spoon, and apple core are just some of their creations that now tower over the world's public spaces.

Pop Revival

The 1980s saw a revival in the form of neo-pop, with Jeff Koons in the U.S. and Ken Done in Australia celebrating popular culture once more. The American Keith Haring made lively pop graffiti on the streets. British Damian Hirst and Japanese Takashi Murakami both work much like Warhol, employing teams to help make their contemporary art.

Look Closer

How does this flowery puppy by Jeff Koons (right) relate to pop art? Think about its scale, materials, and what it represents.

Puppy, Jeff Koons, 1992

Street art by Keith Haring in New York

Making Art Real

Pop's impact on the art world was loud and lasting—it showed that art can be anything, no matter how ordinary, as long as it interests people! It was (and still is) one of the most popular art movements—some Warhols sell for over $100 million now. Pop had a long-term influence on commercial design, and especially on the way we see fine art. Looking outward at the world rather than inward at the gallery, it made art real and accessible for everyone.

Glossary

abstract expressionism—an art movement in the U.S. (1940s–50s) based on creating art for emotional effect, rather than representing something physical

acrylic paint—fast-drying synthetic paint

appropriation—the intentional borrowing or copying of pre-existing images or objects in art

assemblage—an artwork made from a collection of found or gathered objects

Ben-Day dots—a printing technique dating from 1879 that uses widely or closely spaced dots to produce areas of color

canvas—a strong type of fabric that many artists use to paint on

Cold War—a period of hostility between the U.S. and Soviet Union

collaborative—working together

collage—an artwork made by sticking pieces of paper, fabric, or other materials onto a surface

commercial—related to buying and selling things

communist—believing in a classless society, in which property and resources are collectively owned by everyone, rather than by individuals

cubists—artists such as Pablo Picasso and Georges Braque, who made images using geometric shapes and multiple viewpoints (1907–1920s)

Dada—a movement (1916–24) that aimed to destroy traditions in art, with often nonsensical or tongue-in-cheek work

décollage—the opposite of collage; art made by cutting or stripping away pieces of an original image

elitist—seemingly superior to others

emulate—to imitate or follow

Festival of Britain—a national exhibition and fair (1951) that celebrated British industry, arts, and science

icon—a person or thing that is widely admired

immortalize—to preserve something in people's memory

impasto—applying paint thickly so that it stands out from the surface

land art—art made directly in the landscape using natural materials

monochrome—black and white, or using varied tones of a single color

new realism—an art movement (1960–70) that explored "new ways of perceiving the real" and was the European counterpart to pop

op artists—members of a 1960s art movement that used abstract, geometric patterns to create eye-catching optical effects

performance art—when artists act or use their body to create a dramatic form of art

photomontage—a collage made from photographs

photorealists—artists in 1970s U.S., England, and France who painted ordinary scenes with the realistic detail of a photograph

proxy war—a war fought between countries that represent the interests of other, larger powers

replicate—to copy

representational—showing the true physical appearance of things

silk-screen printing—making a print by dragging ink or paint over a stencil marked onto a silk screen

surrealists—members of an art movement (1924–66) that focused on the subconscious mind and the uncanny images of dreams

symbol—a thing that represents, or stands for, something else

texture—the feel of a surface, such as rough brick or smooth glass

typography—the styling of typed letters or words

Venice Biennale—an important contemporary art exhibition held every two years in Venice, Italy

Viet Cong—communist rebels in South Vietnam who fought on the side of the North in the Vietnam War

Vietnam War—a Cold War conflict in which communist North Vietnam defeated non-communist South Vietnam and its American allies

Read More
Books
Richards, Mary. *Splat! The Most Exciting Artists of All Time.* New York: Thames & Hudson, 2016.

Willett, Edward. *Andy Warhol: Fighting to Revolutionize Art.* Rebels with a Cause. New York: Enslow, 2017.

Internet Sites
MoMA Learning: Pop Art
www.moma.org/learn/moma_learning/themes/pop-art

Tate: Pop Art
www.tate.org.uk/kids/explore/what-is/pop-art

Tate: Roy Lichtenstein.
www.tate.org.uk/kids/explore/who-is/who-roy-lichtenstein

(For similar pages on Andy Warhol, Ed Ruscha, David Hockney, Peter Blake, and Patrick Caulfield, replace the artist's name in the URL. Be sure to type in all lowercase!)

Timeline

1912 The cubists Pablo Picasso and Georges Braque invent collage.

1914 World War I begins.

1916 The Dada movement is founded.

1918 World War I ends.

1924 The surrealist movement begins, using unusual image combinations and everyday objects that later inspire pop artists.

1939–45 World War II rages in Europe and beyond. New York takes over from Paris as capital of the art world. Abstract expressionism emerges, focusing on painting inner emotions.

1947 Scottish artist Eduardo Paolozzi starts making collages from commercial imagery. He uses the word "POP!" in one of them.

1950s Acrylic paints become commercially available.

1951 People across the United Kingdom celebrate the Festival of Britain, a showcase of British design and industry after the war. The first color television broadcast is transmitted in the U.S.

1952 The Independent Group (IG) meets for the first time at the Institute of Contemporary Arts, London. Paolozzi delivers his "Bunk!" lecture.

1953 Queen Elizabeth II is crowned in England.

1954 Members of IG start using the term pop art. Neo-Dada emerges in the U.S.—Jasper Johns creates his first *Flag* painting and Robert Rauschenberg develops his Combines. The Vietnam War breaks out.

1956 The IG and other artists collaborate at *This is Tomorrow*, an exhibition on modern life. Elvis Presley has his first number-one hit.

1957 Richard Hamilton defines pop art in a letter to other members of IG. The Soviet Union launches the first satellite into space.

1958 British critic Lawrence Alloway writes an essay called "The Arts and the Mass Media," helping to promote pop art.

1960 New realism is founded in France. John F. Kennedy is elected president of the United States. His campaign posters inspire James Rosenquist to paint *President Elect*.

1961 Soviet cosmonaut Yuri Gagarin becomes the first person in space. Claes Oldenburg opens The Store in New York, selling painted plaster in the shape of food and other goods.

1962 Marilyn Monroe dies. *The New Realists* exhibition unites European and American artists, including Andy Warhol and Roy Lichtenstein, in New York. A symposium is held at the Museum of Modern Art, introducing pop to the U.S. art community. The BBC broadcasts *Pop Goes the Easel*, featuring British artists Peter Blake, Pauline Boty, Derek Boshier, and Peter Phillips.

1963 President Kennedy is shot in Dallas, Texas. The Beatles release their first album. *Six Painters and the Object* takes place at the Guggenheim Museum, New York. Riots erupt in Alabama as people fight for racial equality; using newspaper photos of the event, Warhol makes a series of silk screens the following year.

1964 Rauschenberg wins the grand prize at the Venice Biennale, the biggest art award of the time. *The American Supermarket* exhibition opens in New York. David Hockney visits California and begins making pool paintings. Op art emerges as a style.

1965 Robert Indiana designs his *LOVE* Christmas card for MOMA. Large numbers of U.S. troops are sent to fight in Vietnam.

1966 Pauline Boty dies in London.

1967 The Beatles' *Sergeant Pepper* album is released, with cover art by Peter Blake. The *Homage to Marilyn Monroe* exhibition is held in New York. Britain broadcasts its first color TV program.

1968 Warhol is shot by a radical feminist and nearly dies from his wounds. This takes its toll on pop art as a movement.

1969 American astronaut Neil Armstrong becomes the first person on the moon.

1973 American troops withdraw from Vietnam, having been defeated in the war.

1987 Warhol dies in New York.

1988 Neo-pop artist Jeff Koons makes a sculpture of superstar Michael Jackson.

1997 Lichtenstein dies in New York.

2004 Tom Wesselmann dies in New York.

2008 Rauschenberg dies in Florida.

2011 Hamilton dies in England.

2017 Rosenquist dies in New York.

Index

abstract expressionism, 4, 6–7, 11
action painting, 6
advertising, 4, 8–10, 12–13, 18–20, 37
Alloway, Lawrence, 9
Arman, 15, 27
Axell, Evelyne, 36

Beatles, the, 24–25
Bengston, Billy Al, 21
Blake, Peter, 5, 11, 25, 27, 29, 40
    On the Balcony, 11
Boshier, Derek, 35
    I Wonder What my Heroes Think of the
    Space Race, 35
Boty, Pauline, 27–28, 35, 36
    It's a Man's World I, 36
    The Only Blonde in the World, 27
Braque, Georges, 7
"Bunk!", 8

Caulfield, Patrick, 40–41
    After Lunch, 41
César, 21
Chryssa, 36
Cold War, 34
collage, 5, 7–9, 11–12, 25, 27–28, 36
comic strips, 4–5, 22–23, 29
Cuban Missile Crisis, 35
cubists, 7

D'Arcangelo, Allan, 21, 27
    Marilyn, 27
    US Highway 1, 21
Dada, 7
Dalí, Salvador, 7, 29
Done, Ken, 45
Drexler, Rosalyn, 36

Estes, Richard, 44
exhibitions
    Homage to Marilyn Monroe, 27
    Six Painters and the Object, 30
    The American Supermarket, 30–31
    The New Painting of Common
    Objects, 15
    The New Realists, 15
    This is Tomorrow, 9
Fahlström, Öyvind, 42
    Column no. 4 (IB affair), 42
Festival of Britain, 9

Hamilton, Richard, 5, 8, 10–11, 27
    Interior II, 5
    $he, 10
Haring, Keith, 45
Hirst, Damian, 45
Hockney, David, 5, 40–41, 44
    A Bigger Splash, 40–41

Indiana, Robert, 38–39
    LOVE, 38–39
International Group (IG), 8–10

Johns, Jasper, 7, 31

Kennedy, John F., 12–13, 19, 35
Klein, Yves, 15
Koons, Jeff, 45
    Puppy, 45
Kosolapov, Alexander, 43
    Lenin and Coca Cola, 43

Lichtenstein, Roy, 5, 14–15, 22–23, 27,
    29–31
    In the Car, 22
    Turkey Shopping Bag, 31
    Whaam!, 23
    Woman with Flowered Hat, 29

Magritte, René, 7
Manet, Édouard, 11
Marisol, 37
Monet, Claude, 29
Monroe, Marilyn, 24, 26–28, 43
Murakami, Takashi, 45

neo-Dada, 7
neo-pop, 45
new realists, 15, 21, 42

Oldenburg, Claes, 5, 15–17, 27, 31, 44
    Floor Burger, 16–17
    Floor Cake, 17
op art, 44

Paolozzi, Eduardo, 8–9, 27
    Meet the People, 8
Philips, Peter, 27
Picasso, Pablo, 7, 29
Pollock, Jackson, 6
Pop Goes the Easel, 24, 36
Presley, Elvis, 24, 28

printing, silk-screen, 5, 11, 18–19, 21, 26,
    30–31, 35, 44

Rauschenberg, Robert, 7, 13, 27, 30, 35
    Bed, 7
    Retroactive I, 13, 35
Riley, Bridget, 44
    Hestitate, 44
Rosenquist, James, 5, 12–13, 15, 27, 34–35
    President Elect, 12–13
    F-111, 34
Rosler, Martha, 37
    Vacuuming Pop Art, 37
Rotella, Mimmo, 25, 27
    Elvis Presley, 25
Rothko, Mark, 6
    Untitled (Violet, Black, Orange, Yellow on
    White and Red), 6
Ruscha, Ed, 21
    Standard Station, 21

Segal, George, 32–33
    Gay Liberation, 33
    The Diner, 32
Shinohara, Ushio, 43
    Doll Festival, 43
Space Race, 35
Spoerri, Daniel, 15
    Kichka's Breakfast, 15
Strider, Marjorie, 36
surrealism, 7, 13

The Velvet Underground, 24–25
Thiebaud, Wayne, 14
    Bakery Counter, 14
Tinguely, Jean, 15

Vietnam War, 34–35

Warhol, Andy, 5, 13–15, 18–19, 21, 24, 26,
    29–31, 35, 44–45
    32 Campbell's Soup Cans, 18
    Brillo Boxes, 30–31
    Marilyn Diptych, 26
    Toy Paintings, 29
Wesselmann, Tom, 5, 20, 27–28, 31
    Landscape #4, 20
    Still Life #30, 28
World War I, 7
World War II, 4, 6, 9, 34, 43